**YA BIO AGUILERA**
**Marron, Maggie.**

**Christina Aguilera / by Maggie**
**Marron.**

# christinaAGUILERA

# christin&AGUILERA

by Maggie Marron

UNIVERSE

**For Brett and Jim**

First published in the
United States of America
in 2000
by UNIVERSE PUBLISHING
A Division of Rizzoli
International Publications, Inc.
300 Park Avenue South
New York, NY 10010

2000 2001 2002 2003 2004 2005
/ 10 9 8 7 6 5 4 3 2 1

Printed in Hong Kong

# Contents

There was magic on the set of *The New Mickey Mouse Club* in the 1990s. Everywhere you look, another grad of the show is blazing a trail to stardom: Keri Russell in the top-rated TV show, *Felicity*; Justin Timberlake and JC Chasez breaking hearts in 'N Sync; Britney Spears breaking hearts of her own. . .and now. . .well now there's yet another alum soaring to the top. Five foot two and eyes of blue, Christina Aguilera (that's a-GHEE-lera) may look like a little girl—but oh, can that little girl sing! It's no wonder she's so frequently compared to Mariah Carey and Barbra Streisand.

In 1998, seventeen-year-old Christina made a big splash. First, she got a huge break, signing with Disney to do the soundtrack single "Reflections" for *Mulan*. Then, she signed with RCA to record her first album—and both in the same week. Christina had always known she would be a big star, "ever since I was in diapers," she admitted in an MTV interview. And by August 1999, when her debut album, *Christina Aguilera*, hit the shelves, she realized her dream. The album easily met the record set by Britney Spears earlier that year, and continues selling strong.

Quite possibly the best thing about Christina, though, is her fashion sense. She can get away with wearing the most outrageous outfits and she looks absolutely breathtaking in them. Hot pink is her signature, but she also wears tons of animal prints, leather, plastic—and always with shirts short enough to showcase her pride and joy—that adorable belly button.

Christina Aguilera, the reigning princess of pop music.

Christina blows a kiss to reporters at the 1999 MTV European Awards in Ireland.

But underneath it all, Christina is basically a normal gal. She even sleeps with the lights on because she's afraid of the dark! She loves munching on fast food and spends most of her free time shopping at the mall or seeing movies with her friends. And she even gets all goo-goo-eyed when she meets up with a fellow celebrity—no matter who it is. Take for example the time she met Jay Leno before she did *The Tonight Show*. "I was just upstairs getting my hair done," she gushed to CNN Online, "and Jay comes in, and he's like 'Oh, how nice it is to meet you,' and I was like, 'Oh my God. It's Jay Leno.'"

So what sets this petite powerhouse apart from the other pop stars in her generation? She's got a vast musical background that she just can't wait to explore with her fans. Christina told Lucy Ling during an interview on *The View*, she wants to do more than sing pop music. She'd like to introduce kids to stuff they might not hear every day, music they might not already know, like Etta James or B.B. King. In fact, Christina performed James' "At Last" at the 1999 Lilith Fair. Pretty cool.

Christina is a woman with a mission—no, with lots of missions—and the only place she's going is up! She may be holding her own on the pop charts today, but who knows what the future holds? The former Mouseketeer has been offered tons of film and TV roles, and although she says she wants to stick with singing for now, it isn't hard to imagine that one day she might have her own TV show.

But how did she get her start? What makes her tick? Does her new-found fame come with a price? Read on to find out everything you ever wanted to know about the reigning princess of pop, Ms. Christina Aguilera.

"I've been singing and performing ever since I was in diapers, basically."

-CHRISTINA AGUILERA, MTV INTERVIEW, 1999

Pretty in pink. Christina strikes an adorable pose.

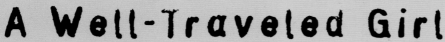

# A Well-Traveled Girl

Christina's fashion sense seems inspired from garment styles around the globe—which is no wonder. If this girl knows anything, it's traveling. It's true. Not many kids could consider the world their hometown, but Christina traveled around so much in her childhood that she's convinced she's probably lived everywhere—from Japan to New Jersey. Traveling hasn't hurt her, however. If anything, it prepared her for the life she was destined to lead—a life of singing and touring and being away from home most of the time.

A child at heart, Christina performs with a cherished teddy bear.

Christina's dad, Fausto Aguilera, is an Ecuadorian-born U.S. Army sergeant. The army changed where he was stationed a lot, so he is the reason the family was always on the road. This didn't bother her mother, Shelly, that much at first. After all, Shelly was no stranger to this kind of life. An Irish-American violinist/pianist, she toured Europe with the Youth Symphony Orchestra when she was just a teenager. Shelly knows first-hand what it is like to live your youth on the road and in the spotlight, but she never discouraged her daughter from pursuing this kind of life for herself. She knew she couldn't stop Christina, even if she tried.

Christina was ready for stardom almost as soon as she popped into the world on December 18, 1980. Her parents were living in Staten Island on that fateful day when they welcomed their first child. Christina was singing before she could talk in complete sentences. "When she was two, I knew what Christina was going to do," her mom told *Rolling Stone Online*. "She would line up all her stuffed animals and sing to them with my little majorette baton. That was her 'ikaphone.' She was too young to pronounce microphone!"

Her childhood is dotted with similar anecdotes. Christina found singing a perfect outlet to deal with the stresses of never living in the same place for too long—a way to deal with making new friends, getting used to a routine, and then being told it was time to pack up and leave everything behind again for the family's next adventure. "I started singing as a love and it was a way that I could release any bad energy, from a very, very young age," she confessed in an America Online chat session. Although her mother has earlier memories, Christina remembers that it was a movie musical that gave her the singing bug; "I started singing from my first inspiration of Julie Andrews in *The Sound of Music*, and I fell in love with it. It's been an ongoing love for a while, and now a career choice."

Christina dons a colorful shawl at the 1999 *Seventeen Magazine* Teen Choice Awards.

## Christina Aguilera
## VITAL STATS

**Full name:** Christina Maria Aguilera

**Birthdate:** December 18, 1980

**Star sign:** Sagittarius

**Birthplace:** Staten Island, NY

# Christina On Stage

"I've always felt the need to be in the spotlight"

-CHRISTINA AGUILERA

# THE SONGS THAT MADE HER FAMOUS

Christina is a fab performer with powerful stage presence. Though she's petite in stature, her amazing voice and love of performing make her sparkle on stage like a gem in a jewelry box. A real trooper in every situation, she gives each performance her all: from her forty-five day, non-stop promotional tour for "Genie," to singing and dancing in the pouring rain for the 1999 Macy's Thanksgiving Day Parade. In a December command performance for President Clinton she warmed the hearts of all, singing "The Christmas Song (Chestnuts Roasting on an Open Fire)" with her idol B.B. King and fellow songstress Jewel.

**"I Wanna Dance with Somebody"**
sung by the baby diva at her first grade talent show

**"The Greatest Love of All"**
Eight-year-old Christina sang this Whitney Houston favorite on *Star Search*

**"I Wanna Run to You"**
recorded in one take on a boombox, this Whitney Houston song landed her the Big Break: a chance to sing "Reflection" for Disney's *Mulan*.

**"All I Wanna Do"**
a duet with Japanese popstar Keizo Nanishi that got Christina international attention

**"Genie in A Bottle"**
her breakthrough Number One hit single

**"What A Girl Wants"**
sealed her destiny as a star with its guitar-driven fun

**"So Emotional"**
a gospel-inspired showcase of Christina's heartfelt style

**"I Turn to You"**
her first ballad, with the power to prove it won't be her last

**"The Christmas Song (Chestnuts Roasting on an Open Fire)"**
Smoky and soulful, and a thrill for Christina when she performed it live with her idol B.B. King for the President and First Lady

In time, constantly moving around seemed to take its toll on the Aguilera marriage. It was one thing to live everywhere when there were no kids-or when the kids were young enough that school wasn't an issue. But that wasn't going to last forever.

When Christina was six, her parents divorced. In a way, this was a good thing. Now, Christina could settle in somewhere, lay down some roots, and build a foundation for her singing career. But divorce is never easy on anyone, especially a small child. And because her father would continue to travel, she wouldn't be seeing that much of him anymore-let alone hearing from him.

Shelly initially headed to Rochester, Pennsylvania, to move back in with her mother. Eventually she chose Wexville, a suburb of Pittsburgh, as the place she would move to with her two young daughters, Christina and Christina's sister Rachel. In Wexville, Shelly met and fell in love with James Kearns, a paramedic, and it wasn't long before they married. Now Christina had a steady residence, a full-time stepfather, and a new stepbrother and stepsister. And within a few years, she'd be the oldest of five kids.

**Christina strikes a pose.**

She may have a number-one selling record, but she's still just a regular girl.

It seemed the perfect American suburban family situation, but how long could a budding superstar live this life of quiet contentment? How long would it be before she started itching to get out in the world again? Christina was always craving something more. "I've always felt the need to be in the spotlight," she told Rolling Stone Online. "But it's a difficult task to be center-stage all the time, especially when there are four other kids needing to be tended to." Even as a child, Christina craved attention: She couldn't get enough of it. "When my family lived in Japan, my mom taught English to this one guy who brought over his paintings," she remembers. "He spread them on the floor and, just to steal the attention away, I started playing hopscotch all over them. I'm just like that."

Okay, so maybe that was bratty, but Christina has always been busting for stardom. She has always wanted all eyes on her and she has always wanted to perform. It got to the point where she was only happy when she was singing. "I've never seen anyone so focused," her mom recalled for Rolling Stone Online. "When she was older, if there wasn't a block party or somewhere for her to sing, she'd get irritable."

But, in a Pennsylvania suburb, just how many opportunities were there for a diva in training? The answer soon became clear, and Shelly Kearns knew it was just a matter of time before her baby would be hitting the road again.

# Christina Is Stylin'!

Christina usually changes her costume several times during a performance, but at this point in the show she looks radiant in a form-fitting, black-sequined, halter-top half shirt. Her hair is blown out straight but remains poofy underneath. How did she get this look? Christina's hair was blown out with a large round brush just before the performance to ensure her hair had extra lift yet still looked totally natural.

## LOOK #1
### Casual Chic

## LOOK #2
### Playing the Crowd

Christina lounging about in some of her most comfortable clothes. A snug-fitting, baby-doll T-shirt in black and white shows off Christina's classic beauty. Satin workout pants are comfortable and elegant at the same time. Christina's hair is left straight, the top partially pulled back in a ponytail. Stylin' shades keep playful wisps from blocking Christina's gorgeous blue eyes.

# CHRISTINA HAS EXCELLENT STYLE.

No style can compare to Christina style: outrageous, elegant, playful, and beautiful. Fire-engine red lipstick and frosty eye shadow against the backdrop of a hot pink shirt and black leather pants that must have been painted on—this babe's got a bod that won't quit and she's always ready, willing, and able to show off!

Sure, she looks like a babe in anything, from casual cargo pants and a baby-doll T-shirt to her snazziest evening wear. But no matter what she puts on, she always manages to show off her adorable belly-button—just like a real genie! Here are some of Christina's fave looks. Try them out for yourself!

## LOOK #3
### A Night on the Town

Christina looked just like she stepped off a catwalk during the Teen Choice Awards. Fuschia is a fave color of this teen queen, and here she proudly proclaims that with a barely buttoned hot pink sweater. Christina's skirt is made of an outrageous lavender animal print plastic. Around her waist she wears a chain of golden medallions to show off—you guessed it! High-heeled shoes give the petite popster extra lift.

## LOOK #4
### Totally Christina

Christina makes a fashion statement at the 1999 MTV Video Awards.

# The Ultimate Christina Quiz

## PART ONE
## Test Your Christina Knowledge

How well do you really know Christina Aguilera? Could you be best pals with her right now—or do you need to read this book a few times really carefully to get your facts straight? Throughout the book, you're going to come across these pop quizzes. Sometimes you can find the answers in the chapter you just read, other times, the answers to the questions will be in other chapters—or maybe not in this book at all! These answers might be found in the notes on her album, or maybe on her official Website. At the end of the book—on page 108—you'll find the answer key. But no peeking! When you get to the end of the book, you'll also be able to score yourself and see how much you really know. Good luck!

# Quiz

**1** **Where was Christina born?**

a   Philadelphia, Pennsylvania

b   Staten Island, New York

c   Rockport, Massachusetts

d   Trenton, New Jersey

e   Atlanta, Georgia

**2** **What musical inspired Christina to become a singer?**

a   *Guys and Dolls*

b   *West Side Story*

c   *Grease*

d   *The Sound of Music*

e   *Rent*

Christina blows a kiss.

**3** What is Christina's fave food? (besides fast food, that is)

a Japanese

b Mexican

c Italian

d French

e Chinese

**4** How old was Christina when she joined *The New Mickey Mouse Club*?

a 12

b 14

c 8

d 16

e 10

**5** Finish this line: "A weaker man might have walked away, but you had faith..."

"I'm not Britney Spears and Britney Spears isn't me. But I think especially when people hear my music.... it'll definitely distinguish who I am."

CHRISTINA IN AN MTV INTERVIEW, 1999

Christina flashes a smile as dazzling as her ensemble.

# Show Biz Beginnings

Even when Christina was a small child, Shelly knew better than to hold her daughter back in her show business ambitions.

A kittenish Christina blowing kisses our way at the 1999 MTV Music Video Awards.

Christina's mom was constantly entering her daughter in one talent competition or another, which Christina always won. When she wasn't performing the talent show circuit, little Christina sang her head off weekends at neighborhood block parties. Wherever there was an open mike, there was Christina. And she made quite an impression on people. As Jode Pohl, director of the Pittsburgh theater company Pohl Productions, remembers, "The thing about her was that she wasn't just a cute little girl with a big little girl's voice. She was a little girl with an adult voice." (*Pittsburgh-Post Gazette*).

At eight years old, Christina got a huge break. She won a spot to compete on the talent show of all talent shows: *Star Search*. Now, not only would she be winning another competition—as she was very sure of herself—she would be doing it on national television! It was a dream come true and an opportunity she was sure would launch her right to stardom.

Christina thought carefully about what song would really show off her vocal abilities. "I sang Whitney Houston's 'Greatest Love of All,' " she told Rolling Stone Online. It was a song she had sung at several events before and she always walked away with a trophy. Besides, Whitney Houston was one of her all-time favorite singers. There was no way she could lose. Or was there?

Sometimes fate works in mysterious ways, and when Ed McMahon read the winner's name after Christina's stellar performance, she burst into tears. She couldn't believe that the boy she had competed against had won. Her mother always taught her to be gracious, however, no matter what happened, so Christina composed herself and gracefully congratulated the winner. "I was told it was fixed but I'm not going to hold a grudge," she told Rolling Stone Online. "I was a good sport about it. My mom made me go back and shake his hand and tell him I was happy he won. Tears were running down my face. Awful." She was devastated by the defeat, but the show must go on, right? Christina picked herself up and went home, determined that she would never be beaten again. And as for the winner—well, who even knows what his name is today.

**Don't let the sign fool you—Christina's not slowing down any time soon!**

## Christina Aguilera
## VITAL STATS

**Hometown:**      Wexford, Pennsylvania
(a suburb of Pittsburgh)

**Home Teams:**      Pirates, Steelers, and
Penguins

**Home-Away-
From-Home:**      *The New Mickey Mouse Club*
and Orlando, Florida

"The day that I'm too good to talk to my fans, or take time to sign an autograph, or give a hug? I don't think that will ever happen."

Having a number-one single and a Top Ten album gives a girl plenty to think about.

As a consolation prize for her *Star Search* effort, Christina won a home sound system. Big deal, right? You bet. Christina used this machine to turn second place into a new opportunity. She continued practicing on the sound system and got herself even more notice when she used it in public. This, combined with her newly found local fame from being on TV, led her to a gig most girls her age couldn't pull off. At ten, Christina started singing the National Anthem at Penguins, Pirates, and Steelers games. She was a regular celebrity in Wexville, but celebrity doesn't come cheap.

One of the drawbacks of Christina's blossoming stardom was that she lost a lot of her popularity at school. "Going to a public school in a small town and not being around kids who did what I did made me feel like an outsider," she told Rolling Stone Online. "I even had to switch elementary schools after *Star Search*. The jealously got really bad. People just felt threatened."

Kids can be cruel, and as her old friends became increasingly jealous of her success, going to school became just unbearable for Christina. You would think her classmates would have fallen all over themselves just to be close to her; instead, they fought to get away from her. They avoided her in the halls, and more and more, she was alone. Ironically, beautiful and talented Christina was the biggest loser at her school—if you can believe that seeing how far she's come today. "You learn the hard way who your friends are," she told Rolling Stone online. "Plus, my circle of friends was the cheerleader clique, so there was already a lot of back-stabbing. It made me introverted."

And it wasn't just her classmates. Her teachers and even her parents' friends jumped on the hate-Christina bandwagon. "As soon as *Star Search* happened, a lot of my mom's friends, other parents, wouldn't talk to us anymore," she told *Teen People*. "Sometimes teachers made it difficult because I would be out with the flu, and I would return to school and the teachers would be like, 'Oh, she wasn't out sick; she was out singing somewhere.'"

Christina had always known that fame had its price, but how high could it be? It was really getting out of hand and she didn't know what she should do. Should she give it all up and pretend to be a normal kid so she could have some happy memories of her teenage years to look back on? "Christina would cry every time she got her name mentioned in the local paper because it would mean more fear at school," Shelly remembered for *Teen People*. "We had threats of slashed tires and her getting beaten up. She would be late to school because I had to time [when we were] leaving the house so there wasn't enough time for them to do things to her."

Eventually, it became unbearable. In addition, her professional schedule was pulling her in so many different directions it was hard to stick to a regular school schedule. The combination of these two factors decided that she would have to be home-schooled. Christina figured someday her classmates and teachers would come around—it was just not the time. Which worked out just fine for Christina. Her career had been blossoming with opportunities. At nine, Christina auditioned for *The New Mickey Mouse Club*, but she was too young to join the cast. She was disappointed but took it in her stride. She knew it was nothing personal and had nothing to do with her talent—and she was right.

Almost two years later, the producers called her back, telling her that they loved her first audition and they could hardly wait until she was old enough to join the cast. Needless to say, Christina landed a role on the same show that would launch the careers of several more young stars, including Justin Timberlake, JC Chasez, Keri Russell, and Britney Spears. "It was a great way to grow up," Christina told CNN Online. "I got the most incredible education in terms of who I wanted to be as an artist and in terms of how the business works. It gave me the focus I needed to make this album."

It was working on MMC that she established an almost immediate friendship with Britney Spears. As the two youngest Mouseketeers, they both looked up to senior cast member Keri Russell. "[Keri] had the big hair and the tight-fitting clothes that were always cute," Christina admitted to Rolling Stone Online. "She was sixteen and could drive and had the cute sports car. It was cute like that."

But Christina and Britney shared more similarities than worshipping Keri: they had both been singing since they were in diapers, they had been entered in constant talent show competitions, they had each auditioned earlier and not made it because they were too young, and both had been on *Star Search*. Although Britney didn't have the same troubles at school, she understood where Christina was coming from. There were both basically small-town girls who were ready for the big time, whether or not their friends understood. Britney was just luckier than Christina that way.

Christina loved her time at *MMC*—well, most of the time that is. "I had to have a pie [thrown at] my face," she told *Teen People*. "That wasn't too fun." No one could ever have predicted the success rate of one-time Mouseketeers, but the girls knew they were lucky to be working with so much talent and ambition. "It was great to be around other kids who were as passionate about their careers as I was," she told Rolling Stone Online
.

But nothing lasts forever. After two seasons featuring the pop-sy twins, *MMC* was canceled. Britney went back home to Kentwood, Louisiana. JC Chasez and Justin Timberlake joined 'N Sync. Keri Russell had already left the previous season to pursue other opportunities. And Christina...well Christina was not about to go back home. Aside from her family, there wasn't really anything there for her, so she embarked on a tour of Europe and Asia. Little did she know that when she got back to the States, her career would really start to take off.

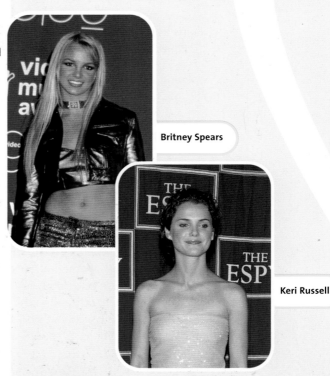

**Britney Spears**

**Keri Russell**

Christina with just a few of her many fans.

# Christina vs. Britney

## BATTLE OF THE BABES

Britney Spears at the
Teen Choice Awards

Christina may have lots in common with Britney Spears—they're about the same age, they both came up in their careers through the same avenues, they both have a great sense of style—but that certainly doesn't mean that they're the same person or that they're trying to accomplish the same things with their careers.

Christina at the opening of the Millennium Village at Epcot Center in Disneyworld

These similarities lead the media to want to stir up controversy in other areas. It's a big headache for both gals that the media have invented these rumors of a rivalry between them. Don't buy into it: they're really great pals. It's true. "[Britney] is completely talented, but we are two different artists," Christina has said over and over again. "People think we cat fight," she admitted to the *Toronto Sun*, "and it's like the minute [her album] *...Baby One More Time* first came out, I seriously was the first in line to buy it. I mean I wanted to support her 'cause she's my friend and I'm sure she did the same thing when my album first came out." They've always been there for each other, ever since they were the babies of MMC.

"[Britney] is completely talented, but we are two different artists"

"Britney is a very talented young lady. And the more people get to know us as artists, you'll get to see how truly different we are."

Both girls have complained about people trying to turn them against each other—or try and take advantage of their friendship by trying to get the answers to pretty private questions. It's true. Christina admits that "even when I'm doing radio interviews and stuff, they want to ask me very personal questions about her, and you have to be a little protective of yourself and what you say because there are so many people wanting to get you to say things and pulling you in so many different directions."

The bottom line is that as long as they're free to do their own thing and be recognized as separate artists with unique qualities to offer, there won't be any problems at all. "There is room for everybody," Christina expressed in an America Online chat session when her album first came out. "Britney is a very talented young lady. And the more people get to know us as artists, you'll get to see how truly different we are."

# Christina Aguilera:
## THE TIMES OF HER LIFE

"You've got to make a decision: Are you going to go down with the situation, or are you going to focus and succeed? My dream of becoming a recording artist kept me going."

—CHRISTINA TO *TEEN PEOPLE*

It's hard to believe that only a few short years ago Christina was sporting mouse ears instead of designer duds.

Christina sure has come far in the past 19 years!

**1980**
Christina is born in Staten Island, New York.

**1981-1987**
Christina lives everywhere on the planet—from Japan to Jersey!

**1987**
Christina's parents split up.

**1987**
Christina, her mom, and her little sister, Rachel, move to Pennsylvania to live with Christina's grandmother.

**1987-1988**
Christina's mom enters Christina in every talent competition under the sun!

**1988**
Christina's mom marries James Kearns and Christina gets a new stepbrother and stepsister.

**1989**
Christina gets a big break—a chance to compete on *Star Search*.

**1989**
Christina loses the competition—a first for her—but knows other opportunities are just around the corner.

**1989**
Christina belts the National Anthem before pro sports games for Pittsburgh teams.

**1990**
Christina tries out for MMC, but she's too young to join the cast.

**1992**
MMC calls back and Christina heads to Orlando with her mom.

**1992-1994**
Christina enjoys her run on MMC, learning how to use her talents and making lifelong friends like Britney Spears.

**1995**
MMC is canceled and Christina returns home.

**1996-1997**
Christina heads to Europe and Asia and causes quite a stir.

**1998**
Christina comes back to the States to try out her pipes on her fellow Americans.

**1998**
Christina is signed by Disney to sing the song "Reflection" for the movie *Mulan.*

**1998**
Christina gets a recording contract with RCA

**1999**
Christina records her first album, the self-titled *Christina Aguilera.*

**1999**
"Genie in a Bottle," the first single off the album, hits the airwaves and blasts off to the number-one position on the charts!

**1999**
Christina hits the talk show circuit, appearing on *The Tonight Show, The Rosie O'Donnell Show, The View,* and others—not to mention making an appearance on *Beverly Hills 90210!*

**1999**
Christina performs "Chestnuts Roasting on an Open Fire" at the White House!

**2000**
"What a Girl Wants" becomes the first number-one song of the new century.

**2000**
Christina wows football fans with a stunning performance at the Superbowl.

**2000**
The singing Christina doll is released—just in time for Valentine's Day!

**2000**
Christina wins a Grammy for Best New Artist and looks forward to a bright future of style, fame, and singing immortality!

# The Ultimate Christina Quiz

## PART TWO
### Test Your Christina Knowledge

Now it's time for part two of the challenge. Remember, some of these questions can be easily answered by reading this chapter. Others will take more work. Of course, if you truly love Christina, you might already know the answers without checking first. Good luck!

**6** Which top star of her own TV show also got her start on *The New Mickey Mouse Club?*

a   Jennifer Love Hewitt

b   Melissa Joan Hart

c   Keri Russell

d   Sarah Michelle Gellar

e   Calista Flockhart

**7** Which eighties pop ballad did Christina sing on *Star Search?*

a   Whitney Houston's "The Greatest Love of All"

b   Prince's "Purple Rain"

c   Madonna's "Crazy for You"

d   Debbie Gibson's "In Your Eyes"

e   Lisa Lisa's "All Cried Out"

**8** What's Christina's favorite sport?

a   Bowling

b   Swimming

c   Basketball

d   Ice hockey

e   Tennis

**9** Who's the president of Christina's fan club?

a   Her sister, Rachel

b   Her father, Fausto

c   Her mother, Shelly

d   Her manager, Steve

e   Her friend, Britney

**10** Finish this line:
"There's a heart that must be free to fly..."

"My dream has always been to record an album before I was out of high school."

—CHRISTINA AGUILERA, *PITTSBURG-POST GAZETTE*

Christina hit the bull's-eye with her smash hit single, "Genie in a Bottle."

# High E Above Middle C

If Christina was looking to regroup for a while when she headed overseas for a post-MMC tour, she was in for a surprise. It wasn't that she didn't expect what the various countries she visited had to offer. After all, considering her childhood, Christina was by this time a seasoned traveler. Actually, it was that the diminutive diva caused a surprise stir overseas, which took her a bit off-guard. At home, she had enjoyed her time in the spotlight and minor celebrity as a Mouseketeer—but a superstar? Maybe not in the States just yet, but when she touched down on foreign shores, they were ready for her.

It's obvious that Christina is at her happiest—and most electrifying—when she performs.

Years earlier, American actors David Hasslehoff of *Baywatch* fame and Alyssa Milano, who was best known at the time for her role as Samantha in *Who's the Boss?* and who, today, bewitches audiences as Phoebe in *Charmed*, had both hit the big time on the European-Asian pop scene, while over in the States, no one even knew they could sing. In the mid 1990s, pop music ruled Europe and Asia. Audiences could not get their fill of acts like the Backstreet Boys and 'N Sync. So when Christina arrived, pop fans were primed and ready to meet the latest American sensation, the tiny girl with the booming voice.

Christina hardly took a day off. In Japan, she teamed up with Asian pop superstar Keizo Nakanishi to record a duet for "All I Wanna Do," for which they performed on tour together and taped a video. Christina was playing to sold-out arenas in Asia, while in her home country she had yet to record or release even a single. At the Golden Stag Festival in Romania, a big-name-boasting musical event, Christina was mobbed by 10,000 fans when she innocently waded into the crowd. She also managed to upstage the festival's top acts, including Sheryl Crow and Diana Ross.

Christina's middle name might be Maria, but "Sassy" would be equally as appropriate.

## Christina Aguilera
## VITAL STATS

**Hair:** Blonde
**Eyes:** Blue
**Height:** 5' 2"
**Heritage:** Ecuadoran and Irish-American
**Trademarks:** Cropped-tops, navel gems, and white blonde hair with a sexy zigzag part.

"I love girlie things, like going shopping."

Despite a grueling schedule of interviews and public appearances, Christina always manages to remain fresh as a daisy.

Yep, she was big overseas. The combination of her undeniable beauty, her incredible fashion sense, and overwhelming talent won over foreign audiences who adored her in MMC that much more. And the attention she received started to make American record executives take notice. Before she left for her tour, her manager, Steve Kurtz, sent a demo to RCA Records. They were really impressed by what they heard and Kurtz was sure that Christina would come home to a recording contract.

Back home in early 1998, Disney contacted RCA looking for a female voice to record the main song "Reflection" for their newest production, *Mulan*. A&R Director Ron Fair was blown away by Christina's demo tape and immediately recommended that they try her out. Christina was ecstatic just to have the opportunity to audition. After all, Disney just didn't give their songs away to anyone—and seldom would such an opportunity go to a basically unknown

ex-Mouseketeer. Vanessa Williams, yes. Elton John, absolutely. Christina Aguilera—Christina who? It was completely unprecedented, but the door was opened to her. She may have been given the in, but it was pure talent that landed her the gig.

And now for the catch. The song, written by Matthew Wilder and David Zippel, featured a note combination that was nearly impossible for even the strongest singers to clinch. It called for the performer to sing a high E above middle C—an acrobatic musical feat and what Christina will always remember as "the note that changed my life" (*Providence Journal*).

Christina wasn't nervous at all. She broke out the sound system she won from *Star Search* and made a tape of herself singing Whitney Houston's "I Wanna Run to You." Even though she had turned up second best with Whitney before, she had faith that this time Whitney would pull her through. And she was right. Steve Kurtz sent the tape to Disney via FedEx, and within 24 hours, she won the gig. Twenty-four hours after that, they had recorded the song and Christina was ready for the next opportunity.

It was just that easy. Christina learned the song, rehearsed it, and recorded it all in one day. She was ready to take the next flight home when she realized they were going to set her song against the backdrop of a full-fledged orchestra. She could not miss that! "It's enough to bring tears to my eyes, hearing a 90-piece orchestra playing your song," she remembered for the *Pittsburg-Post Gazette*. "It was amazing."

"Reflection" hit the Top 15 on the A/C charts and Christina enjoyed the success of the song by bouncing around on the talk show circuit and singing her hit live on shows like *The Donnie & Marie Show* and *CBS This Morning*. The song also clinched a Golden Globe nomination for Best Original Song in a Motion Picture. Christina was proud to perform the song for what has become one of her favorite Disney movies. "The song's theme—the struggle to establish your identity—was something I could really relate to as a teenage girl myself," Christina told MTV Online.

Christina was riding high on her new accomplishment—until she got some other good news. Apparently RCA was ready to sign a fresh new female singer who had just emerged from a glorious tour of Europe and Asia—that would be Christina. How thrilling! First the Disney deal and now a record deal! It was more than she ever could have imagined for herself at this age. She dreamed of recording an album before she finished high school and now that would become a reality. Christina was on her way.

A pensive Christina takes a well-earned break before heading back to the spotlight.

## Christina Luvs?????

Carson Daly

She may be the busiest artist on the recording circuit today, but a gal's gotta find a little time for romance in her schedule, right? If we could set Christina up with any hottie, who would the lucky guy be?

There was speculation that Christina had a little crush on MTV's *Total Request Live*'s Carson Daly. In fact, Carson's break-up with *Time of Your Life* star Jennifer Love Hewitt was blamed on an out-of-control mutual attraction between Carson and Christina. Now, while both parties are flattered, each denies the allegations. As Christina told *Teen People*, "My first reaction was, 'Oh, I'm important enough to be gossiped about.' Then I was like, 'Oh, no! This isn't true!'"

He may be adorable, but Carson seems a little too clean-cut for our girl. She needs a guy with an edge—a guy she can share fashion tips with! That's it! How about A.J. McLean of the Backstreet Boys? He's always up to something wild and crazy and he loves to change his style—as often, it seems, as he changes his underwear! Couldn't you just see them out on the town together, wearing matching fuschia animal-print tops... Well, I guess we're going to have to keep dreaming on that front. "I like the bad boys," she confided to *Teen People*. But, "If I were to date someone, I'd rather date a rocker than a boy-band guy."

A.J. McLean

Eminem

A rocker... Hmmm. Let's see. Well, how about a rapper? Christina has admitted on more than one occasion to being attracted to bad-boy Eminem. She even ran it by Rolling Stone Online during an interview: "Eminem and I would make a cute couple, no?" Well, they surely would make an adorable couple, but sorry, girlfriend. This man is totally taken. Not only did he recently get married—he's also a dad. We'd better move on!

How about a fellow Latino? Ricky Martin is single these days and looking finer than ever. Who could say no to him when he shakes that adorable bon-bon? Or maybe Enrique Iglesias is the right guy for Christina. She's certainly never been shy to admit how she feels about him.

But hey—most importantly, let's not rule out her fans! It's okay to dare to dream, guys—but if you want to win over this babe, you've got to keep your cool! As Christina told Rolling Stone Online, "It's cute to have guy groupies, but some of them get out of hand." So send as many love letters, photos, gifts, and poems as you dare—but give this babe some space.

# Only time will tell who Christina gives her heart to. . .

Ricky Martin

Enrique Iglesias

"I was thrilled to be working with so many great producers on this album," Christina told MTV. And surely she was working with a stellar cast. "Genie in a Bottle" was penned by David Frank and Steve Kipner, the same guys who wrote "The Hardest Thing" by 98°. Diane Warren, famous for huge hits like Aerosmith's Grammy-nominated "I Don't Want to Miss a Thing" from the *Armageddon* soundtrack, wrote "I Turn to You." "Love for all Seasons" and "Love Will Find a Way" are the contributions of Carl Sturken and Evan Rogers, who have also produced a number of hits for 'N Sync and Boyzone. Travon Potts, who co-wrote Monica's "Angel of Mine," wrote "Blessed" for Christina. But as good as the songs looked on paper, they needed that most important of finishing touches: a singer who could pull them off. The writers had no complaints. Diane Warren has said that "Christina is just the greatest singer. When she hits those high notes, you can really feel her talent."

No contradictions from her record company for that. "She is a badass genius of singing," Ron Fair beamed to Rolling Stone Online. "She was put on this earth to sing, and I've worked with a lot of singers—the O'Jays, Natalie Cole, Dianne Reeves. When Christina met with us, she didn't care that she was auditioning for a record deal; she got into a performance zone that you see in artists much more mature than she is, like a k.d. lang."

You would think that with all this great chemistry, actually making the album would be smooth sailing, but anything that comes out as good as Christina's first album is destined to hit a few bumps in the road. At first, Christina was over-singing her songs, especially "Genie." "I wanted to start belting with the first verse," she told *Entertainment Weekly*, "and [executive producer Ron Fair] did teach me how to not let the cat out of the bag too soon, how to keep it soft at first." That way, the song would build and tease listeners, leaving them anxiously awaiting the next note.

Glamorous as it seems, even making a hit record can get tedious at times. "You'll mess up, and things will happen, and you'll have to start over," Christina told the *Pittsburg-Post Gazette*. "After singing and singing and singing, it just gets so tiresome."

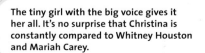

The tiny girl with the big voice gives it her all. It's no surprise that Christina is constantly compared to Whitney Houston and Mariah Carey.

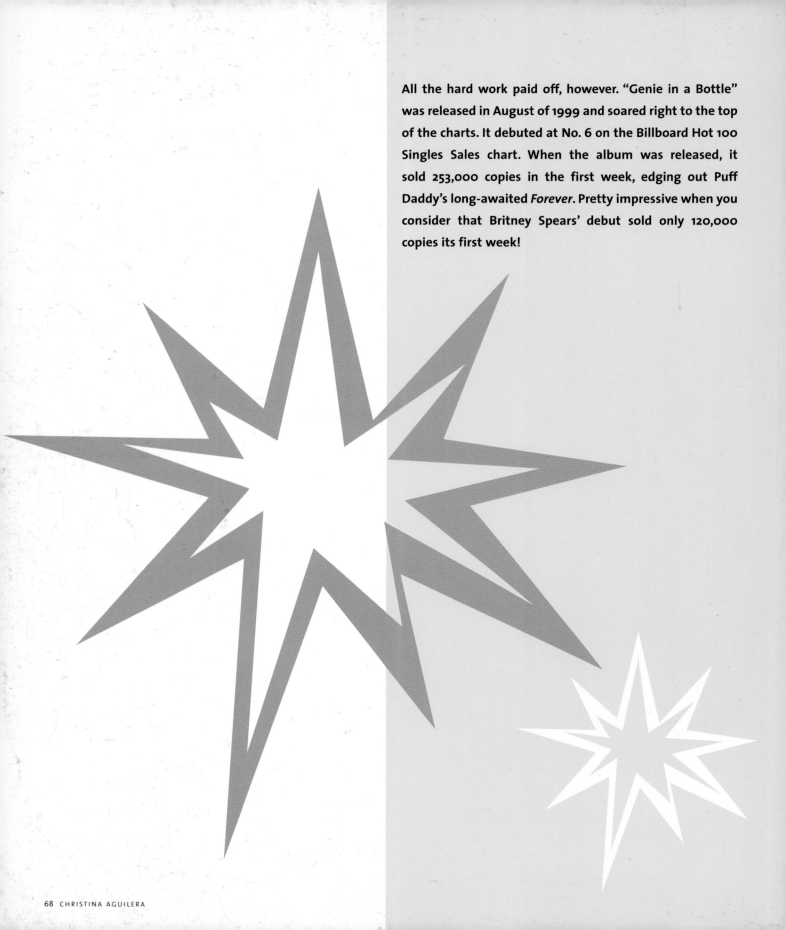

All the hard work paid off, however. "Genie in a Bottle" was released in August of 1999 and soared right to the top of the charts. It debuted at No. 6 on the Billboard Hot 100 Singles Sales chart. When the album was released, it sold 253,000 copies in the first week, edging out Puff Daddy's long-awaited *Forever*. Pretty impressive when you consider that Britney Spears' debut sold only 120,000 copies its first week!

Christina just loves those bad boys—such as Tommy Lee, her co-presenter at the 1999 MTV Music Video Awards. Watch out Pammy!

# The Ultimate Christina Quiz

## PART THREE
### Test Your Christina Knowledge

So you're ready for a new challenge. Okay, well the same rules
apply in this quiz so get focused and start answering!

**11** What was the name of the hit single Christina recorded with Japanese pop star Keizo Nakanishi?

a  "I Will Always Love You"

b  "In the Name of Love"

c  "All I Wanna Do"

d  "Once Bitten"

e  "Young American"

**12** How old was Christina when she was signed to sing "Reflection" for Disney's *Mulan*?

a  11

b  13

c  15

d  17

e  19

**13** What onetime teenage American actress had also been a pop sensation in Japan?

a  Jennie Garth

b  Alyssa Milano

c  Melissa Joan Hart

d  Tracy Gold

e  Kelly Martin

**14** What's Christina's littlest brother's name?

a  Michael

b  Stanley

c  Arnold

d  Jack

e  Frank

**15** Finish this line: "When I lose the will to win, I just reach for you..."

"It's time for something different. It's time that music makes kids feel confident and secure. And I'm looking forward to reaching out and touching as many of them as possible."

-CHRISTINA AGUILERA, CNN ONLINE

Though only 5'2", Christina's stage presence is larger-than-life.

# I Dream of Genie

By August of 1999, "Christina Aguilera" was a household name, thanks to a supposedly provocative single that you just can't stop singing once you catch it on the radio. "It's a dream come true that people are responding in such a positive way to my music," she gushed to Billboard. "At first, I was a little afraid that some people might not completely get where I'm coming from—particularly with 'Genie in a Bottle.'" She certainly had every right to be afraid. Christina wasn't thrilled about the song at first. "To tell the truth," Christina admitted to MTV, "I don't know if I should say this...but I didn't want to release 'Genie in a Bottle' as my first single."

It was the lyrics of the song that initially made Christina uneasy. She thought people would misunderstand them, and therefore, misunderstand who she was and where she was coming from.

Christina is a role model because she exudes a confidence well beyond her nineteen years.

Not surprisingly, Christina has gotten some flak for the seemingly suggestive lyrics and seductive tone of "Genie in a Bottle." She's very quick to clear up any misunderstandings, however. As she insisted to CNN Online, "[The song is] not about sex. It's about self-respect. It's about not giving in to temptation unless you are respected." Which makes a lot of sense when you think about the words. "You've got to rub me the right way"—well, when you "rub someone the wrong way," it's usually because you've done something to them they see as disrespectful, so if you rub someone the right way...see, you get it. Then, you play on the genie theme, and rubbing a lamp to get the genie to come out, and it all comes together. "I thought the whole idea was very cute," Christina has admitted.

Whatever it's about, the song has catapulted her to fame—in September of 1999, Christina became RCA's first number-one female solo vocalist in five years! "Seeing my name in the No. 1 spot on the Billboard chart has always been a dream of mine," she told CNN Online when she found out that she had clinched the top position.

So how did she get so hot so fast? RCA promises that it wasn't by over-publicizing her. "We didn't spend any more on Christina than we would to launch any other artist," Jack Rovner, executive vice president and general manager of RCA Records has admitted. "It was enough to get it started." It was pure talent—not to mention impeccable style.

And fans will have lots to look forward to as more and more Christina singles get released. There really is something for everyone, and that's what they intended with this album. "With my record, we tried to make something that would appeal to the teen market, which is really hot right now with acts like Britney Spears and 'N Sync," she told Launch.com. "But we also wanted to bring in a mature and older audience as well, and I think we've got a really good balance on this record with the up-tempo songs as well as the ballads." For lovers of a good ballad, there's "I Turn to You" or "Blessed." When you're in the mood for something a little bouncy, there's "What a Girl Wants" and "Come On Over (All I Want Is You)."

At the opening of Epcot Center's Millenium Village, Christina proves that she's a star for the next century.

## Christina Aguilera
# VITAL STATS

| | |
|---|---|
| **Parents:** | Fausto Aguilera, and Shelly and James Kearns (stepfather) |
| **Siblings:** | Rachel, Michael, Stephanie, and Casey |
| **Show-biz Friends:** | Justin Timberlake, JC Chasez, Keri Russell, and Britney Spears |
| **Best Buds:** | Christina's dancers—Nick Aragon, Buddy Mynatt, and Jorge Santos—and, especially, her mom Shelly and little sister Ro. |

# What a Girl Wants, What a Girl Needs...

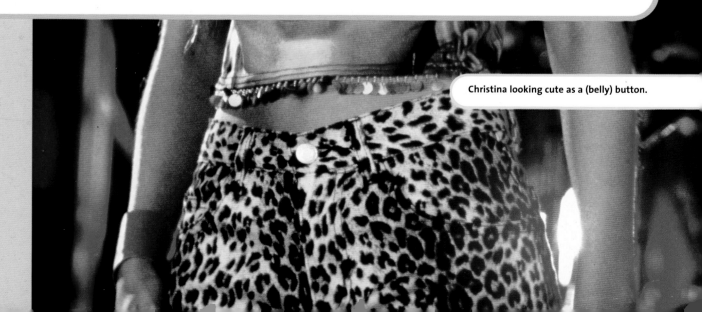

Christina looking cute as a (belly) button.

Christina grew up loving *The Sound of Music*. It was her first inspiration to become a singer herself. Of course, "whiskers on kittens, warm woolen mittens, and brown paper packages tied up with string" can only take a girl so far, right? Move over Julie Andrews, here are some of Christina's favorite things.

### Favorite colors:
Fuchsia, turquoise, and black

### Favorite sports:
Ice hockey, baseball, volleyball

### Favorite foods:
Mexican, steak, and fast food

### Favorite musicians:
Etta James, Madonna, Mariah Carey, Whitney Houston, Michael Jackson, Eve 6, Boys II Men, Brian McKnight, No Doubt, Julie Andrews, B.B. King, Limp Bizkit

### Favorite Disney movies:
*Mulan* and *The Little Mermaid*

### Favorite school subjects:
English and math

### Favorite holiday:
Christmas

### Favorite celebrities:
Enrique Iglesias, Ben Affleck, Johnny Depp, Julio

"So Emotional" allows Christina to explore a very important musical influence of hers. "R&B is a big part of me," she told *Gavin*. "When I was 7 or 8 I used to take B.B. King guitar tracks and just riff over them. I was really into Billie Holiday and gospel and I really think those influences show in 'So Emotional.'" And let's not forget the two songs we love so much already: "Genie" and "Reflection."

Variety is really important to Christina. "If music becomes too pop, I lose interest," she told *Time* magazine. Down the line, the label plans to expose other sides of Christina. "It will be as if she's growing up, by virtue of the singles we put out," Rovner says. "You need an introduction and to be embraced by a fervent fan base, so we went with the more youth-oriented song, but ultimately we'll be getting to the big ballads."

In addition to showcasing her vocal talents, Christina has made a name for herself with her wardrobe. In a few short months, she's turned fashion around. Buyers have been falling all over themselves to offer Christina-style outfits in their clothing stores. Hot pink is back in a big way! And by the way, how cool were those pants she wore in the "Genie" video—come on! "Everybody seems to love those," she admitted in an American Online interview. "They're from Abercrombie and Fitch...and you actually don't get to see the coolest part which is on my lower left pant leg by my calf. There's this huge dragon, which is so cool. But you all seem to still like them, so it's kind of cool." You bet we love 'em, Christina—now where did you say we could buy 'em?

Christina's been getting lots of exposure for those great styles lately. It seems like every time you turn on the tube, there she is! In addition to a guest appearance on *Beverly Hills 90210*, she's been on all the big talk shows. "It's crazy," she has admitted. "I get to do [some] of the biggest shows on TV—Leno, Rosie! Plus, I'm doing a show with the Backstreet Boys for their fall tour in the States as well."

Though a runner-up on *Star Search*, these days
Christina is shining brighter than ever.

A seasoned globe-trotter, Christina shimmers in an Eastern-flavored outfit.

Christina's at the top of her career, but sadly, the problems at home have only gotten worse, believe it or not. She really felt the sting in May of 1999 when she attended her high school prom. "I wasn't going to, because I knew I would be treated a little different," she told *Entertainment Weekly*, "but finally I called my friend Marcy and said, 'Let's just have fun with this. Set me up with a really cute blind date.' But then a friend of mine was hurt because he wanted to go with me, so I ended up having two dates for the prom!" You can't go wrong with two dates, right?—or can you?

Although it helped ease the uncomfortable tension for her between her and the other girls at the prom, she was still treated like the plague. "I got along better with the guys than the girls," she continued to *Entertainment Weekly*. "Only two girls came up to talk to me. Later I found out they were telling their boyfriends, 'If you talk to her, I'll kill you'....It's always rough with that high school thing." Will she ever win the love and respect of the girls she grew up with? This is something poor Christina has to deal with every time she goes home. "All I want to do is be normal," she told *People Weekly*. "But really, it's other people who won't let me be that way."

Still, Christina knows she would never be happy living the normal life. As she continued to *People*: "If I was in school now, I'd be looking out a window thinking 'What if I'd gone out there to pursue my dream?'" There are no "what-ifs" for Christina anymore.

Tatyana Ali is pretty in pink.
A two-piece gown shows off her killer bod.

Christina Aguilera might be five feet, two inches with a tiny frame, but you'll never lose this petite beauty in a crowd. Her fashion flare sets her apart. Shimmer and shine define her on-stage, often with enough grown-up-worthy glamor to make her look super sultry! Although she can play it fresh and natural like any teen, Christina is unafraid to try extremes, from knock-out glam to hip casual. She likes to play and experiment with outrageous fabrics and textures: plastic, beaded fabrics, animal prints, feathers, and fluff. On any given day, you may find her cool and casual in soft paisley-printed pants one minute, and a quick-change later, in a sexy, hip-hugging long skirt with a tiny cropped top.

Although she has droves of imitators, she's the innovator. Fitting for the genie she is, her clothes make magic with flashes of metallic thread, and glimmers of gold, silver, and sequins. As for colors, the hotter the better. Christina's light hair and complexion glow when she wears hot pink—a real favorite. Turquoise, another beloved Christina-hue, really brings out her gorgeous eyes.

Britney Spears, though often cute and casual, shows her golden girl side.

She likes things to be snug, and with a bod like hers, no worries. Everyday loves include baby doll tees, soft cropped sweatshirts, spaghetti strap tanks, and long, side-slit skirts with funky shoes. Whatever her fashion mood, Christina's clothes are soooo cool. How does her style compare to other top babes? Check out these fashion-forward stars.

Jennifer Love Hewitt in a delicate, two-toned pink and white gown.

Brandy turning heads in a taupe gown that shows off her excellent curves.

Keri Russell, an early influence on Christina, is almost regal here in a powder blue gown.

# The Ultimate Christina Quiz

## PART FOUR
### Test Your Christina Knowledge

Christina's mega hit, "Genie," made magic on the charts. If you've been singing it, hopefully some of that stardust has rubbed off on you—here's the next part of the test.

**16** What famous songwriter penned Christina's ballad, "I Turn to You"?

a   Diane Warren

b   Babyface

c   Max Martin

d   Matthew Wilder

e   Steve Kurtz

**17** What was one of Christina's favorite subjects in school?

a   Home economics

b   Chemistry

c   History

d   English

e   Spanish

**18** What is Christina's mother's maiden name?

a   Kearns

b   Fidler

c   Broccoli

d   Fulton

e   Jackson

**19** Who does Christina thank first in the acknowledgments of her album?

a   Her mom, Shelly

b   Her stepsister, Stephanie

c   Her manager, Steve Kurtz

d   The Lord

e   Britney Spears

**20** Finish this line: "There are times that test your faith, 'Til you think you might surrender..."

"I can't really picture me doing anything else besides what I'm doing now. I don't know [what else I'd be doing], but something funny. I always wanted to work the window at a drive-thru fast food restaurant. I always thought it was a cool thing to do."

-CHRISTINA IN AN *MTV* INTERVIEW, 1999

Looking every inch the glamorous movie star at the Disney American Teacher Awards.

# Out of the Bottle

Christina Aguilera is on top of the world, every day soaring further and further away from the animosity of the small-town kids who never understood her. With looks like hers, plus her insatiable drive, powerful pipes, and style, the only way for Christina to go is up.

As far as Christina's personal life goes—well, what personal life? She doesn't have a boyfriend right now because her career is too demanding. She is by far one of the most dedicated singers blazing the charts today. Just ask anyone who's worked with her. "I've worked with the Artist and Ricky Martin...Christina's the hardest-working person I've ever met," said Nick Aragon, one of Christina's dancers, to *Teen People*. "She gets this look on her face, almost like a glare, and I know not to go near her because she's so focused."

Proud of her Hispanic heritage, Christina hopes to one day record a Spanish-language album.

## Christina Aguilera
## VITAL STATS

**First Hit Single:** "Genie in a Bottle"
**Record Contracts:** RCA
**Manager:** Steve Kurtz
**Musical Influences:** Etta James, B.B. King, Billie Holiday, Mariah Carey
**First Tour with a Group:** TLC
**First Christmas Single:** "The Christmas Song (Chestnuts Roasting on an Open Fire)"

Christina making a big impression at
Sound Republic in London.

One short-term goal Christina has is to learn to speak Spanish fluently. Although she doesn't have a lot of contact with her real dad, she's very in touch with her Ecuadoran heritage. "My mom went to college to be a translator, so it was spoken in my house, and I understand the majority of the Spanish language," she told *Teen People*. "That is something I'm going to work on." Her mom still prepares lots of ethnic dishes she learned to make from her ex-husband's mother. A major goal for Christina to learn the language is to record her album in Spanish for her father's side of the family. "It's important that it be authentic, not a wannabe Latin album."

Christina has lots of plans, but first and foremost, she wants to take her singing career as far as she possibly can. She doesn't want to be a flash in the pan. She'd like to evolve, like her biggest idols, Madonna, Mariah Carey, and Barbra Streisand—and hopefully start rubbing elbows with them. As she said in an America Online chat, "I would love to work with [Mariah Carey] one day, as well as Madonna. She's wonderful and continues to reinvent herself, so those are two people I'd like to work with."

In addition to her singing and learning Spanish, what else will she be up to? "I plan on going out there and making a great impact on the world!" she voiced to Launch.com. "No, seriously, I plan on venturing out into all different kinds of fields in this business and not just singing, but that's my main love right now and hopefully we'll see what the future brings."

# There's Something About Christina...

"We're all hooked on 'Genie in a Bottle' like there's no tomorrow, but who'd'a thunk that Christina Aguilera's whole debut album would turn out to be so darn good?.... Girlfriend can sing."

—Kim Patrick, *Seventeen* Online

"Move over Mariah—this Genie's bound to make some chart magic."

—*Mademoiselle*, July 1999

"...don't think BRITNEY, think WHITNEY, because this canary-in-training has a big booming voice that needs no mixing desk crutches in order to impress....If a big future doesn't immediately materialize for this girl, there's a conspiracy in effect somewhere."

—mtv.com

"Look for . . . listeners to devour this delicious pop treat."

—*Billboard,* July 1999

"She comports herself like a pro, as if she were born with a mike in her hand, donning platform booties."

—Anthony Bozza, *Rolling Stone,*
October 1999

"One of the most strikingly gifted singers to come along since Mariah Carey."

—*Time* magazine

One of Christina's goals is to keep evolving both as an artist and as a person.

Christina will be touring with the Backstreet Boys—and no doubt, she'll have her own US tour soon. "The studio can be confining. I need to be challenged," she told *Time* magazine. Lucky for Christina, she has a voice that's just as powerful live as it is in the studio, so she has the freedom to perform wherever and whenever she wants. And her record label is not going to prevent her from pursuing whatever opportunities come her way. Ron Fair says RCA will "not shackle" Aguilera. He sees her doing TV and even Broadway someday. "She's our Streisand," says Fair.

Eventually, Christina admits that she'd like to move into acting, but it's important for her right now to establish herself as a lasting singer. "I'm very interested in acting, but right now I'm busy promoting my album and going on tour because that's my first love, but I'm very interested in doing some parts that may come my way," she disclosed in an America Online chat session. "I've been offered a few movie parts so far, but I have to really concentrate on singing. But it's something I'm interested in doing eventually. I haven't been offered a part that truly inspires me to take time off, though."

And time off is not something this babe is looking for right now. There will be plenty of time to rest later—yeah, like when she's eighty! Right now, she's enjoying the rush. She lives all over the place, but her most steady residence is a Manhattan apartment. As she confessed to *Gavin*, "...it's crazy, but fun. When I recorded the album I was living in a hotel room in L.A., and I recently moved into my first apartment in New York. Right now, I'm bouncing back and forth across the country like a ping pong ball." She also spends a lot of nights in her fixed-up basement apartment of her mother's Wexville home.

But what her future holds is up in the air from minute to minute. "Right now I'm playing it by ear," she said in an America Online chat. "I'm going to ride this amazing trip that I'm taking in my career that seems to be blowing up...all the way." And what about what the rest of the kids her age are up to right now? "...college is something I want to do but probably not major in music, but maybe psychology...".

Whatever path Christina decides to take, the glow of her talent and determination will always shine through. Whether she plays the glitter girl, music-career girl, or down-to-earth girlfriend, the spell of the genie is with us to stay.

"I've always envied people who had best friends they've known since they were little, because I've never had that. I'd have to keep picking up and moving."

-CHRISTINA TO *TEEN PEOPLE*

Christina has her own unique brand of "grrrl" power.

Do Your Make-up Just Like Christina!

# CASUAL

When Christina is just hanging out, preparing to spend a day at the mall, she wears her makeup in a subtle fashion. Over a lightly applied foundation, Christina wears just the slightest amount of blush for a hint of color. Her eye make-up is always spectacular—no matter what her plans for the day. Here, blue mascara and just a touch of frosted eye shadow around the eyes have a sparkling daytime effect. Top it off with frosty pink gloss on her lips and voila!—playtime Christina comes to life!

Christina always looks great, whether she's just hanging out or belting her heart out in front of thousands of fans. Her make-up is a staple of her look. **Try these techniques out for yourself!**

# PERFORMANCE

Christina in full performance mode. Notice how dramatic her eye make-up looks in this setting. Dark black eyeliner and frosted grays and purples work best to show off Christina's baby blues way back to the very last row in sold-out auditoriums. Your best bet is to use a liquid black eyeliner to achieve this effect. However, if you only have an eyeliner pencil to work with, melt the point by burning it over a lit match for a few seconds. Allow it to cool for a few more seconds, then apply. Always apply eyeliner just below your bottom eyelashes. This will give the illusion that your eyes are bigger than they actually are. To top it all off, Christina wears frosted silver-lilac polish on her perfectly manicured nails.

# EVENING

When she isn't on stage, Christina wears her make-up more toned down. She keeps the dark eyeliner—an absolute staple of her look—but applies it on with a lighter hand. The same goes for her unique eye-shadow technique.

# The Ultimate Christina Quiz

## PART FIVE
### Test Your Christina Knowledge

Okay, you're finally at the home stretch. Once you've answered
these questions, you'll be ready to score yourself and see how well
you really know Christina!

**21** What famous boy act will Christina soon be touring with?

a     The Backstreet Boys

b     98°

c     The Moffats

d     Aaron Carter

e     Take Five

**22** Where is Christina's main residence?

a     Los Angeles

b     Boston

c     New York City

d     Philadelphia

e     Las Vegas

**23** At the Lilith Fair 1999, Christina sang "At Last." Which singer initially made that song famous?

a     Ella Fitzgerald

b     Etta James

c     Diana Ross

d     Barbra Streisand

e     Gladys Knight

**24** Christina's stepfather is a:

a     physician

b     policeman

c     paramedic

d     lawyer

e     postal worker

**25** Finish this line: "You take me high and low, you know..."

# The Ultimate Christina Quiz

Okay, put your pencils down and fold your hands on your desk. The big test is over. Now you can check out the answers and see how you did. And hey—no cheating.
No matter how you did, there's always going to be more Christina to know!

## ANSWERS

**PART ONE:** b,d,b,a, "...strong enough to move over and give me space." ("What a Girl Wants")

**PART TWO:** c,a,d,c, "...that burns with the need to know the reason why." ("Reflection")

**PART THREE:** c,d,b,a, "...and I can reach the sky again." ("I Turn to You")

**PART FOUR:** a,d,b,d, "...and baby I'm, I'm not ashamed to say that my hopes were growing slender." ("Blessed")

**PART FIVE:** a,c,b,c, "...I'm never sure which way you're gonna go, you're such a mystery to me." ("So Emotional")

## Scoring

So, how well do you really know Christina? Give yourself the correct number of points for each question that you answered.

| If you answered... | ...then give yourself this many points |
|---|---|
| **#1** | |
| a | 3 |
| b | 4 |
| c | 0 |
| d | 2 |
| e | 1 |
| **#2** | |
| a | 3 |
| b | 1 |
| c | 2 |
| d | 4 |
| e | 0 |
| **#3** | |
| a | 1 |
| b | 4 |
| c | 3 |
| d | 2 |
| e | 0 |
| **#4** | |
| a | 4 |
| b | 3 |
| c | 0 |
| d | 1 |
| e | 2 |
| **#5** | |
| If you guessed the line | 4 |
| If you knew the song it came from | 2 |
| If you drew a complete blank | 0 |
| **#6** | |
| a | 3 |
| b | 2 |
| c | 4 |
| d | 1 |
| e | 0 |
| **#7** | |
| a | 4 |
| b | 0 |
| c | 3 |
| d | 2 |
| e | 1 |
| **#8** | |
| a | 0 |
| b | 2 |
| c | 3 |
| d | 4 |
| e | 1 |
| **#9** | |
| a | 3 |
| b | 0 |
| c | 4 |
| d | 1 |
| e | 2 |

#10

| If you guessed the line | 4 |
|---|---|
| If you knew the song it came from | 2 |
| If you drew a complete blank | 0 |

#11

| | |
|---|---|
| a | 3 |
| b | 2 |
| c | 4 |
| d | 0 |
| e | 1 |

#12

| | |
|---|---|
| a | 0 |
| b | 1 |
| c | 3 |
| d | 4 |
| e | 2 |

#13

| | |
|---|---|
| a | 1 |
| b | 4 |
| c | 3 |
| d | 0 |
| e | 2 |

#14

| | |
|---|---|
| a | 4 |
| b | 3 |
| c | 2 |
| d | 1 |
| e | 0 |

#15

| If you guessed the line | 4 |
|---|---|
| If you knew the song it came from | 2 |
| If you drew a complete blank | 0 |

#16

| | |
|---|---|
| a | 4 |
| b | 1 |
| c | 2 |
| d | 3 |
| e | 0 |

#17

| | |
|---|---|
| a | 0 |
| b | 1 |
| c | 2 |
| d | 4 |
| e | 3 |

#18

| | |
|---|---|
| a | 3 |
| b | 4 |
| c | 0 |
| d | 2 |
| e | 1 |

#19

| | |
|---|---|
| a | 3 |
| b | 1 |
| c | 0 |
| d | 4 |
| e | 2 |

#20

| If you guessed the line | 4 |
|---|---|
| If you knew the song it came from | 2 |
| If you drew a complete blank | 0 |

#21

| | |
|---|---|
| a | 4 |
| b | 3 |
| c | 2 |
| d | 1 |
| e | 0 |

#22

| | |
|---|---|
| a | 2 |
| b | 1 |
| c | 4 |
| d | 3 |
| e | 0 |

#23

| | |
|---|---|
| a | 2 |
| b | 4 |
| c | 1 |
| d | 3 |
| e | 0 |

#24

| | |
|---|---|
| a | 1 |
| b | 3 |
| c | 4 |
| d | 0 |
| e | 2 |

#25

| If you guessed the line | 4 |
|---|---|
| If you knew the song it came from | 2 |
| If you drew a complete blank | 0 |

## REPORT CARD
NOW, ADD UP YOUR POINTS AND SEE HOW WELL YOU KNOW CHRISTINA!

### 0-25 points
**D**

Time to hit the books. Hey, have you been paying attention or not? Apparently, there's a lot you still need to learn about Christina. So re-read this book. Visit her official Website. Do whatever you can to improve your knowledge—then take the test again!

### 26-50 points
**C**

Okay, not bad. But I know you can do better. You know the basics about Christina— but really, there's so much more you can know! Try to think like Christina. Go to the mall and buy an outfit she would wear. Get your head in the right place and try taking the quiz again when you're all dressed up and ready to go.

### 51-75 points
**B**

Getting better. Give yourself a hand. You're pretty much on the mark with what you know about Christina, but you could definitely know more. Go back through this book and skim through the information. And a visit to Christina's official Web site might not hurt either!

### 76-100 points
**A**

Hooray! You're at the head of the class in the Christina Aguilera school of knowledge. But don't think just because you got an A here, you know everything there is to know about Christina. She is a gal in constant motion, always evolving as a performer and a person. So check out those magazines and Websites—and keep learning!

Even at her most low-key, Christina's charm is high-wattage.

# For the Fans

*"My fans are so cute"*
—CHRISTINA AGUILERA

Christina may have crushes, but her heart belongs one hundred percent to her fans. She has said over and over that one of the best things about her newfound fame is meeting and talking with her fans. She is truly grateful to her listeners, and, although this genie has finally gotten her wish for the spotlight, she has stayed REAL. Fans connect with Christina's genuine spirit, a spirit that is just as powerful as her incredible voice. With her dazzling songs, and fab lyrics, Christina sends a heartfelt message to her audience: Be strong, follow your dream, and believe it can all come true.

Christina's rise to stardom may look like pure magic, but she is one hardworking baby diva! A few of her rare song tracks trace her footsteps across live performances, television shows, and sound stages from the U.S. to Japan. Girlfriend is BUSY.

## RARE CHRISTINA TRACKS

"Genio Atrapado"
(Spanish version of "Genie")

"Reflection" live track
(for *CBS This Morning*)

"Genie in a Bottle" live track
(for MTV's *Total Request Live*)

"So Emotional"
(for MTV's *Total Request Live*)

"Genie in a Bottle"
(UK Dance remix)

"All I Wanna Do"
(duet with Japanese pop star Keizo Nakanishi)

# Write to Christina

**Christina Aguilera Fan Club**
**244 Madison Avenue**
**Suite 314**
**New York, NY 10016**

**Christina Aguilera**
**c/o RCA Records**
**1540 Broadway**
**New York, NY 10036**

**Email: Christinaaguilera@mailcity.com**

# WEB SITES: OFFICIAL

www.peeps.com/christina

www.Christina-A.com

# COOL WEB SITES: UNOFFICIAL

www.diversebeats.com/christina/

http://fly.to/christina_a

www.geocities.com/christinaasite/

There's lots more where that came from. Your best bet is go to one of your favorite search engines, like Yahoo or Lycos, type in Christina's name, and a whole world of Chistina Aguilera will be open to you. Here's a tip: log on with your 'rents when you want to search this stuff out. There's a lot of phoney baloney on the Web and your folks can help you get past all that and into the good stuff! Also, put her name in quotes ("Christina Aguilera")—that way, you are sure to get the best of the best.

**For Christina Aguilera Merchandise:**

**www.ChristinaA.howfun.com**

Is friendship between you and Christina in the stars?

Use the chart below to see whether you might be soul sisters or not-so-best friends.

| | Capricorn | Aquarius | Pisces | Aries | Taurus | Gemini | Cancer | Leo | Virgo | Libra | Scorpio | Sagittarius |
|---|---|---|---|---|---|---|---|---|---|---|---|---|
| Capricorn | ✹ | ☹ | ☹ | ☺ | ✹ | ☹ | ☺ | ☺ | ✹ | ☹ | ☺ | ☹ |
| Aquarius | ☹ | ✹ | ☹ | ☹ | ☹ | ✹ | ☹ | ☺ | ☹ | ✹ | ☹ | ☺ |
| Pisces | ☹ | ☹ | ✹ | ☹ | ☺ | ☹ | ✹ | ☺ | ☺ | ✹ | ☺ | ☹ |
| Aries | ☺ | ☹ | ☹ | ✹ | ☺ | ☺ | ☹ | ✹ | ☹ | ☺ | ☺ | ✹ |
| Taurus | ✹ | ☹ | ☺ | ☺ | ☺ | ☹ | ☺ | ☺ | ✹ | ☺ | ☺ | ☹ |
| Gemini | ☹ | ✹ | ☹ | ☺ | ☹ | ✹ | ☹ | ☹ | ☺ | ✹ | ☹ | ☺ |
| Cancer | ☺ | ☹ | ✹ | ☹ | ☺ | ☹ | ☺ | ☺ | ☺ | ☹ | ✹ | ☹ |
| Leo | ☺ | ☺ | ☺ | ✹ | ☺ | ☹ | ☺ | ✹ | ☹ | ☹ | ☺ | ✹ |
| Virgo | ✹ | ☹ | ☺ | ☹ | ✹ | ☺ | ☺ | ☹ | ✹ | ☹ | ☹ | ☹ |
| Libra | ☹ | ✹ | ☺ | ☺ | ☺ | ✹ | ☹ | ☹ | ☹ | ☺ | ☺ | ☹ |
| Scorpio | ☺ | ☹ | ✹ | ☺ | ☺ | ☹ | ✹ | ☺ | ☹ | ☺ | ☺ | ☹ |
| Sagittarius | ☹ | ☺ | ☹ | ✹ | ☹ | ☺ | ☹ | ✹ | ☹ | ☹ | ☹ | ✹ |

# Christina In the Stars

CAPRICORN

AQUARIUS

PISCES

ARIES

TAURUS

GEMINI

CANCER

LEO

VIRGO

LIBRA

SCORPIO

SAGITTARIUS

# KEY

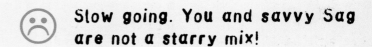 Slow going. You and savvy Sag are not a starry mix!

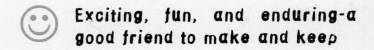 Exciting, fun, and enduring—a good friend to make and keep

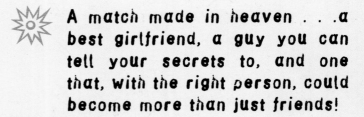 A match made in heaven . . .a best girlfriend, a guy you can tell your secrets to, and one that, with the right person, could become more than just friends!

> "This is like my dream and it's finally becoming a reality. It feels so good."
>
> -CHRISTINA IN HER VIDEO, *GENIE GETS HER WISH*

# Wishing on a Star

Usually it's the genie that grants the wishes, but in this case, the tables have been turned. Christina has had three big wishes for her career—and all of them have come true!

For as long as she can remember, Christina has always wanted to be a singer. Alacazam! That's wish number one. Christina has been enjoying living this wish every day of her life since she was just a little kid.

Christina's second big wish was to record an album before she graduated from high school. Kablam! Not only had Christina recorded *Christina Aguilera*, but the "Genie in a Bottle" single catapulted to the top of the charts while her old high school chums were sporting their caps and gowns!

As for the third wish, Christina was just dying to have a number-one album, which was no problem once the bottle was uncorked and everyone got to know just who this pretty little genie was. *Christina Aguilera* sold 253,000 copies its first week out and hit the number-one position within a matter of weeks.

Perhaps the only wish this chart-topper has these days is to meet that someone special she can hang out with, going to movies or hitting her fave fast-food joints. For now, her schedule is so demanding, it seems all she can do is wish. "My work is my boyfriend," she chuckles. "It's awful."

If there's one thing this girl loves to do, it's performing. And why not—she's so good at it! Christina and her four guy dancers put on an electric show, whether they're playing in the States, in Europe, or even Japan!

There's no doubt who the star of the show is, but Christina knows how important her guys are. Not only do they make her look great on stage, they're also her really close pals. It's hard to be on the road all the time. Christina gets really lonely sometimes for her mom and her little brother Michael, especially. It's a good thing she gets along so well with the guys, whether they're in front of a crowd, deciding on costumes, planning their dance moves, or running to make another plane.

When Christina dresses for a performance, she makes sure to wear clothes comfortable enough to dance around in, but sexy enough to have all eyes on her. For her dancers, she makes sure the guys look great, but also that they won't sweat to death in their stylish duds.

Before they put on a show, Christina and her dancers make it a point to all join hands and say a silent prayer together. Then, the guys bound out to the stage and warm up the crowd for their leading lady, who paces back and forth in the wings. By the time Christina makes her way into the spotlight, the crowd is usually going so crazy that they won't even hear the first few notes Christina sings over their cries of "Christina's number one!"

Christina is a natural. In fact, she's never had any formal vocal or dance training—which is hard to believe when you watch those killer moves or listen to her belt her heart out, but it's absolutely the truth! "I had no real vocal training," she admitted in her video, *Genie Gets Her Wish*. "It was all basically from listening to records and really, like, loving what I listened to, and picking up all sorts of sounds and techniques and things, and creating my own sound so it's, like, cool."

# Performance Crazy

# Christina Diary

Here is a place to record your true thoughts. If you are honest, some of the answers you write down may surprise you! Whether you're Christina's greatest fan, or someone who just likes Christina, the diary is a fun way to find out what you REALLY think about things. What are your Christina faves? Talent? Looks? Clothes? Are the two of you alike—or WAY different? Would your friends love you or hate you if you started stylin' a-la-Christina? Is there advice you would share with her if you were buds? Secrets you would tell? Go ahead—write it all down here—secrets, thoughts, dreams or doodles. We won't peek!!!!

## SONGS

Fave Christina song?

What song do you wish she would record?

Do you remember where you were when you first heard "Genie"?

Fave Christina video?

Which Christina songs do you know by heart?

If you had a chance to perform any of her songs on MTV, would you do it?

Which song would you pick?

If you dedicated a Christina song on the radio, which one would you dedicate, and who would you dedicate it to?

Name a Christina song that best describes your life.

Name one that best describes your fave friend. One that describes who you're crushin' on?

## STYLE

If you could be Christina for a day, what would you do?

What is your favorite thing about her? Least favorite?

Give Christina a makeover—using other stars for inspiration—would she look better with Britney's hair? With Keri's curls?

If you could make ONE thing about yourself exactly like one thing about Christina, what would change?

Should Christina try acting? What shows would she be good in? What should her character be like?

Would you choose the same shows for yourself? The same character?


## CRUSH

Who do you think Christina would make a cute couple with?

Would the person you chose for Christina be the right guy for YOU, too?

If you're crushin' on a guy already, do you think Christina would like him?

Christina asks you for dating tips—what do you tell her?

If you had to choose one of Christina's outfits to wear on a first date, which one would choose?

Choose a line from a Christina song that describes a fave thing about your crush?

# Bibliography

PERIODICALS

Bronson, Fred. "Christina Aguilera's First Wish: A No. 1." *Billboard*. (July 31, 1999): 106.
_____. "Garth 'Gaines' Pop Breakthrough at 'Lost.'" *Billboard*. (September 11, 1999): 110.

Campbell, Kevin. "Who's Next? Top 40's Next Wave." *Gavin*. (April 18, 1999).
"Christina Makeup Tips: How to Get That Genie in a Bottle Look." *Entertainmenteen*. (December 1999): 41.

Croghan, Tara. "Move Over Britney—The Genie's Out of Her Bottle: Christina Aguilera's self-titled album is a wish come true." *Teen Celebrity*. (December 1999): 26-29.

Jamison, Laura. "Heavyweight." *Teen People*. (December 1999/January 1999): 92-98.

Gardner, Elysa. "Blush of Young Talent Waiting in the Wings." *USA Today*. (February 23, 1999).

Gregory, Sophronia Scott and Hayes Ferguson. "Uncorking the Genie: Ambitious and talented singing sensation Christina Aguilera becomes a teen player." *People Weekly*. (September 27, 1999): 75.

Mayfield, Geoff. "Her Wish is Fans' Command." *Billboard*. (September 11, 1999): 108.

Pietroluongo, Silvio. "Bottle Rocket." *Billboard*. (July 10, 1999): 95.

_____. "Hot 100 Singles [Spotlight.sub.TM]." *Billboard*. (July 31, 1999): 99.

Smith, Andy. "Budding Talent." *Providence Journal-Bulletin*. (August 27, 1998). Sodergren, Rebecca. "The Right Note: Wexford Teen Lands RCA Records Contract And A Deal To Sing Hit Song For *Mulan*." *Pittsburg Post-Gazette*. (July 30, 1998). "Song." *People Weekly*. (September 6, 1999): 45.

Thigpen, David E. "Christina's World: A new teen star has a voice that goes way beyond mere kid stuff." *Time*. (August 16, 1999): 69.

Willman, Chris. "'Bottle' Rocket: teen queen Christine Aguilera gets her wish: two prom dates, a chart-topping album, and "Genie in a Bottle," a soaring single." *Entertainment Weekly*. (September 17, 1999): 31.

BOOKS
Robb, Jackie. *Christina Aguilera: An Unauthorized Biography*. New York: HarperCollins, 1999.

WORLD WIDE WEB

"Absolute Christina Aguilera: Bio." MTV Online.
Azzarelli, Ally. "Christina Aguilera's Got It Goin' On." Music.com.
"Bio." Peeps.com.
Boehlert, Eric. "Christina Aguilera, Puff Daddy Displace Backstreet Boys, Limp Bizkit." Rolling Stone Online. (September 1, 1999).
Bozza, Anthony. "The Christina Aguilera Story." Rolling Stone Online.
"Christina Aguilera: Genie In A Bottle 'MTV Interview.'" MTV Online (1999).
Flick, Larry. "Christina Aguilera Expands Beyond 'Genie.'" Billboard Online. (July 20, 1999).
Patrick, Kim. "New Releases for August 24." Seventeen.com.
"The Princess Bride." mtv.com. (May 1999).
"The Sounds of Summer's Newest Pop Stars." mademoiselle.com (July 1999).
Sylvester, Sherri. "Aguilera Unbottled." CNN Online. (September 16, 1999).
"Wall of Sound Review: Christina Aguilera." Wallofsound.com.
"Web Celeb Christina Aguilera." Yahoo.com.

And kudos to the following Web sites and providers for having such great information:
Cdnow.com, America Online, hiponline.com, Launch.com, pop.com, Teen Magazine Online, Vibe Magazine Online, YM Online,

# ACKNOWLEDGMENTS

There are so many people that go into making a great book, it sometimes seems unfair that only the author gets credit on the front cover. For this effort, many players participated in making it the work of art is has become and I am thankful to all of them. Most prominently among them, I'd like to thank Shawna Mullen, my editor, who helped me make this book sing. Without her incredible talents and dedication, this book would not have turned out as fab as it has. And thank you to Elizabeth Smith at Universe Publishing who signed the project up. I also want to thank book designer Leeann Leftwich, for her wonderful design and superhuman speed. Double kudos to Jonathan Ambar for his help and pop culture genius. Not to be forgotten are the people in my personal life who gracefully handled even my most stressful moments in the writing of this book: my awesome parents, siblings, and auntie, my wonderful friends and business partner, and the way cool guy I share my life with.

## ABOUT THE AUTHOR

Maggie Marron is a New York-based freelance writer and editor. She is the author of *Britney Spears: Stylin'*, *Ricky Martin*, *The Backstreet Boys*, and *Will Smith: The Greatest*. Maggie profiles celebrities for several Websites and magazines, including People Magazine Online. Write to Maggie with your comments and questions or suggestions for future books at: maggiemarron@chickmail.com.

# PICTURE CREDITS

**All Images used with permission**

**Images courtesy of London Features International (USA) Ltd:**

| | |
|---|---|
| Front cover: | Jen Lowery |
| Gregg De Guire | pp. 14, 16, 27 upper, 30, back cover, left |
| Jen Lowery | pp. 17, 21, 95 |
| Lawrence Marano | pp. 12, 28, 76, back cover, right |
| Ilpo Musto | pp. 20, 22, 23, 26 lower, 27 lower, 44, 56 |
| Ron Wolfson | p. 80 |

**Images courtesy of Retna Ltd. NYC:**

| | |
|---|---|
| Bill Davila | pp. 32, 33, 38 upper, 43, 62, 63 lower, 69, 83, 98 |
| Armando Gallo | pp. 59, 96, 110 |
| John Gladwin | pp. 53, 65, 92 |
| Steve Granitz | pp. 18, 40, 47, 60, 61, 63 upper, 73, 82, 84, 88, 90, 104 |
| Walter McBride | pp. 24, 25, 34, 36, 41, 42, 54, 74, 118 |
| Leo Sorel | pp. 26 upper, 39 |
| John Spellman | pp. 38 lower, 85 |
| Kelly Swift | pp. 66, 72, 103 |
| Barry Talesnick | pp. 52, 79, 100 |